A Student's Guide to the Study of History

———

John Lukacs

ISI Books

Wilmington, Delaware

A Student's Guide to the Study of History is made possible by grants from the Lee and Ramona Bass Foundation, the Huston Foundation, Barre Seid Foundation, and the Wilbur Foundation. The Intercollegiate Studies Institute gratefully acknowledges their support.

Lukacs, John, 1924–

    A student's guide to the study of history / by John Lukacs—
    Wilmington, Del.: ISI Books, 2000.

        p. ; cm.
        ISBN: 1-882926-41-2

      1. History. 2. Historiography. I. Title. II. Series

D208 .185 2000   00-66794
909—DC21   CIP

ISI Books
3901 Centerville Road
Wilmington, DE 19807
www.isibooks.org

Cover and interior design by Sam Torode

Manufactured in the United States of America

A STUDENT'S GUIDE TO
THE STUDY OF HISTORY

THE PRESTON A. WELLS JR.
GUIDES TO THE MAJOR DISCIPLINES

EDITOR
Jed Donahue

⁊⁖

PHILOSOPHY   *Ralph M. McInerny*

LITERATURE   *R. V. Young*

LIBERAL LEARNING   *James V. Schall, S.J.*

THE STUDY OF HISTORY   *John Lukacs*

THE CORE CURRICULUM   *Mark C. Henrie*

U.S. HISTORY   *Wilfred M. McClay*

ECONOMICS   *Paul Heyne*

POLITICAL PHILOSOPHY   *Harvey C. Mansfield*

PSYCHOLOGY   *Daniel N. Robinson*

CLASSICS   *Bruce S. Thornton*

AMERICAN POLITICAL THOUGHT   *George W. Carey*

RELIGIOUS STUDIES   *D. G. Hart*

THE STUDY OF LAW   *Gerard V. Bradley*

NATURAL SCIENCE   *Stephen M. Barr*

MUSIC HISTORY   *R. J. Stove*

CONTENTS

An Introduction—To Yourself   1

The History of History   7

Professional History   23

The Methods of History   26

The Interest in History   32

The Greatness of Historical Literature   36

STUDENT SELF-RELIANCE PROJECT:
Embarking on a Lifelong Pursuit of Knowledge?   48

AN INTRODUCTION—TO YOURSELF

※

WHAT is history?

No definition will do. Earlier in this century, two German historians tried to give such definitions. They were ludicrous, running to sixty words or even more. They remind us of Dr. Johnson's great saying: "Definitions are tricks for pedants." Ha! I just wrote: *remind.* And that *re-minds* me, instantly, of another great Johnsonian saying: that we (teachers or, indeed, everyone) are here less to instruct people than to remind them. Re-mind: to think, and to become conscious, of something that we already know—even though we have not been thinking about *that* in *this* way.

A good description—a description, not a definition*— is this: "History is the memory of mankind." Now,

---

* Note, already at this point, that *descriptions* are more telling than are *definitions.* For such is the nature of human language and of human thinking. Try to "define" such things as "beauty" or "truth" or "straight." We all know what they are—without their definitions. Yes, "straight is the shortest possible distance between two points." A child does not

memory—every kind of memory—is enormous, just as the past is enormous. (The past is getting bigger every hour, every day.) But it is not limitless. There is the entire past. There is that portion of it (a varying portion, but let that go for a moment): the remembered past. And there is a yet smaller portion of that: the recorded past. For a long time—and for many professional historians even now—history has been only the recorded past. No, it is more than that: it is the remembered past. It *does* depend on records; but it is not merely a matter of records.

But this is true of every human being. You have your own history, because you have your own past—ever growing and ever changing*; out of this past surges your memory

---

know that definition, but he knows what *straight* is. Definitions are the sometimes necessary, surely in natural-scientific matters, instruments for accuracy. But historical knowledge is marked by the aim of understanding, even more than of accuracy, though not necessarily at the expense of the latter. History is always *descriptive*—and, by necessity, never *definitive*.

* It is not only the *quantity* but the *quality* of your past that changes. Suppose that something happened to you today, something bothersome, of which you can remember the smallest details. A few years pass. You recall that day—forgetting many of its details—and may say to yourself: "Why was I so upset about *that*?" (Or: "Why had I not noticed *that* then?") The *quantity* of details of that day has waned; but the *quality* of your understanding of what had happened increased.

of your past; and here and there exist some tangible records of your past. I am coming to your records in a moment, but, first, a few matters about memory.

All human thinking—conscious *and* unconscious—depends on memory. There is no function of the human brain that is not connected with memory. For a long time neurologists thought that memory was a very important part of the brain, but only a part; their present tendency is to recognize its central function. (Even our dreams are inseparable from memory: it may be said that when we dream we do not think differently; we only remember differently.) If our memory ceased we could not go on living; we would, for example, walk through a window instead of through a door, not knowing—more precisely, not recalling—that *this* is a window and *that* is a door. As the great Christian thinker Søren Kierkegaard said: "We live forward, but we can only think backward."

One more thing about the past. The past is the only thing we know. The present is no more than an illusion, a moment that is already past in an instant (or, rather, a moment in which past and future slosh into each other). And what we know about the future is nothing else than the projection of our past-knowledge into it. We know that it will get dark at night, because it has always been so. Notice, too, that even in "Science Fiction" the author puts himself at a point from which he relates the fabulous events he describes *backward*—that is, he writes in the past tense. The reason for this is that the human mind cannot for long sustain attention to a narrative that is composed in the future tense. In sum: our sense of the past is profoundly inherent in the functioning of our minds.

Socrates said that all knowledge must come from human knowledge and from knowledge of the self: *Gnothi se auton*—Know Thyself. (Shakespeare: "To thine own self be true.") What this also means—and what it has come to mean (about this condition, see later)—knowing yourself means knowing *your* own history, your own past. This knowledge of the past is the very opposite of a burden—a good example of how the function of the human mind differs from the functions of matter. By *knowing* something our mind may or may not be enriched; but it may be *eased.** Of course memory may be inaccurate and even fal-

---

* Two examples: (1) Someone gives you an address or a telephone number, which is 1776. An added piece of your knowledge but also something that *eases* your mind: it is easier to remember, since you *already* know the number 1776. (2) Psychoanalysis, when it is reasonably applied (which is not always the case), may *ease* the patient's mind by

lible. But human memory is inevitably historic, to some extent. Your grandfather tells some of his experiences during World War II; their content is historical at least in some ways and to some extent. In sum: it is not only the history of mankind that is the remembered past; so is everybody's, including your own.

But then you may ask: My grandfather keeps telling us this fabulous story about the war. And he always talks so much. How much of *that* is true? But one day he brings out a newspaper clipping from *Stars and Stripes*, reporting the exciting capture of that German armored train by Battalion C, Company A, of the 28th Division—his division. That printed record seems to *confirm* the Grandfather Story. (That this newspaper story may be sensationalist or inaccurate is another matter—that, too, we must leave for a moment, except that your eye may be caught by something slightly disturbing therein: your grandfather's name is misspelled in it, and his hometown is wrong.) And here I get to the matter of *records*. Aren't they what history *is?* Yes or, rather, no:

---

making him recall, on a conscious level, something that he had suppressed or forgotten: a welcome *addition* to his consciousness. (In other words, the very opposite of the case of a pebble in our shoe: we know that it is a pebble, and we want to throw it away.)

because history is something more than mere records. But—and that is *the* important point—your own records are historical, too. Yes, you don't have many of them. There is your high school yearbook; a few ticket stubs; some photographs; in your mother's cupboard, a few old postcards; and, lo, there is a letter from your great-grandmother describing her honeymoon trip to Havana in, say, 1924. Well, *all* of these are historical records, not only because their very shape or form or color or scent vitalizes one's memory and imagination. In that letter of your great-grandmother's the handwriting is old-fashioned, spiky; the paper has yellowed, and the ink has faded; they bear marks of the past, of *a* past: but there is more to that. That plain old letter is *as much of a historical record* as, say, a typescript record of a cabinet meeting of the Eisenhower presidency. As a matter of fact, *more* of a historical record. Why? Because the record of that cabinet meeting was probably drafted and typed by a secretary, without President Eisenhower's seeing it, and perhaps even without his signing it.* But your great-grandmother's letter was handwritten, by herself. Even if it contains a few

---

* The last presidents who wrote—some of—their own speeches, and who signed—most of—their letters and documents by hand, with a fountain pen, were Franklin Roosevelt and Harry Truman.

routine phrases such as "wish you were here," it is genuine and authentic. And it is the authenticity, the genuineness, of every human document—of every human expression—that counts.

In sum: your great-grandmother was as much of a historical person as was President Dwight David Eisenhower; and her remnant "records" are but one proof of that. In sum: there is no difference between a historical source and a "non-historical" source, because there is no difference between a "historic person" and a "non-historic person." (Shakespeare, in *Henry V*: "There is a history in all men's lives.") Let me reformulate this: All men's lives are historic. It is not only that there is *some* history in their lives. They are components of the history of their times.

Now, this is a relatively recent recognition. Let us now see how we got there.

THE HISTORY OF HISTORY

æ

EVERYTHING HAS its history, including history. And in the history of mankind we can see a certain evolution: from historical being to historical thinking and then to historical consciousness.

Let us begin by asserting what is unquestionable: only human beings are historical beings. All other living beings have their own evolution and their life span. But we are the only living beings who *know* that we live while we live— who know, and not only instinctively feel, that we were born and that we are going to die. Animals and other living beings have an often extraordinary and accurate sense of time. But we have a sense of our history, which amounts to something else.

This sense of history—in other words, the knowledge that we are historical beings—is detectable in some of the oldest human records and achievements left to us from the most ancient of cultures. It is there in the Bible, in the Old Testament. There, unlike in other mythological scriptures, is a mass of material that is not only spiritual or exhortative but historical: accounts of men and women and places and events that have since been proved by archaeology and by other evidence. Yet the Old Testament often combines history and legend*; that is, material or genealogical informa-

---

* Note that the word *legend* originally meant "something that ought to be read." (The history of words—their original meaning, their eventual changes—is often the surest key to the history of human thought, for there is no thinking without words. "In The Beginning Was The Word"—not the number, or the image.)

tion on the one hand, and symbolic descriptions of people and events on the other. The New Testament—that is, the life of Jesus Christ—is *more* historical. Consider the very words of the Gospel of St. Luke, Chapter 2:

> And it came to pass, that in those days there went out a decree from Caesar Augustus, that the whole world should be enrolled. / This enrolling was first made by Cyrinus, the governor of Syria. / And all went to be enrolled, every one into his own city. / And Joseph also went up from Galilee, out of the city of Nazareth into Judea, to the city of David, which is called Bethlehem: because he was of the house and family of David. To be enrolled with Mary his espoused wife, who was with child. / And it came to pass, that when they were there, her days were accomplished, that she should be delivered. / And she brought forth her firstborn son, and wrapped him in swaddling clothes, and laid him in a manger; because there was no room for them in the inn....

This description—or account—is exactly and thoroughly *historical*. There is nothing even remotely comparable to that in the accounts of the coming of other gods or founders of religions, whether Greek or Roman or Oriental. Unlike other founders of religions *before* him, Jesus Christ was a historical person. For believing Christians he was not *only* a historical person of course, but that is not our argument here. The historicity of Jesus Christ (which we may regard as God's great gift to mankind) is incontestable: there exist Jewish and Roman and other sources about the fact of his existence, though not of course of all his deeds and sayings (or of their meaning). The very writing of St. Luke is marked by the evidence of something new at that time: of *historical thinking*.

However—in this sense St. Luke had his forerunners. They were the Greeks. As in so many other instances, the Greeks were the creators of many of the fundaments of our entire culture and civilization. Among them we find the first examples of historical thinking (and, therefore, of historical writing)—indeed, the very word "history," which in ancient Greek meant something like "re-search." The three greatest classical Greek historians were Herodotus, Thucydides, and Xenophon. It is interesting to note that all of them wrote something like contemporary, or nearly contemporary, history about events and people that they knew and that they had witnessed. (Xenophon had marched with ten thousand Greek soldiers across Anatolia—today's Turkey—to the sea and described that in his book *Anabasis*, that then became near-immortal.) Herodotus was sometimes called the Father of History: he was a man of the world, and perhaps his most lasting achievement was the ease and the clarity of his style.* But for our purposes here, running through the history of history, perhaps the most telling achievement is that of Thucydides. In the Introduction to his *History of the Peloponnesian War* he asserts his purpose. This war is not yet over, he writes: but there are already so many false stories of this event or that, of this man or another, that he is compelled to tell what really happened. This search for the truth—which most often consists of the reduction of untruths—is the essence of historical research: a fabulous achievement of the Greek mind. There is also Thucydides' conviction of the permanent value of history. He hoped, he wrote, that his *History* would be read "by those who desire an exact knowledge of the past as a key to the future, which in all probability will repeat or resemble the past.** This work is meant to be a permanent possession, not the rhetorical

---

* Note: there can be no good historian who cannot write well. That is not simply a matter of style. Writing well means thinking well. If you cannot tell a story clearly, this means that it is not really clear in your own mind.

** We have to be careful with this phrase. In this matter—perhaps only in this matter—we have become more sophisticated than Thucydides. A very similar and oft-cited sentence was that by the fine American philosopher George Santayana: "Those who do not know history are condemned to repeat it." This is a poetic formulation, full and rich in meaning, while not definitely precise. We are not "condemned" to

triumph of an hour."

And now we must note that for the next two thousand years (Xenophon, Thucydides, Herodotus all lived in the fifth century B.C.), there was no profound change in the nature of *historical thinking*. Important and readable historians existed during the Roman Empire, the Dark Ages, and the Middle Ages; but their achievements, though often considerable, were not very different from those of the Greeks. At least the names of Tacitus or Livy or even Julius Caesar (who "made" history as well as wrote it) must be known to you. There were many others—Polybius, Plutarch, Procopius, Symmachus (necessarily a very incomplete list)— Roman and Byzantine and Christian historians, writers in the Middle Ages. Let us pause, if only for a minute, at Plutarch, who is eminently readable.* He was a biographer.

---

repeat our mistakes: repeating them, we condemn ourselves. More important, history does not exactly repeat itself, but historical circumstances, and human inclinations, do. This happens not only because of the passage of time, but also because of God's miraculous creation to the effect that no two human beings are ever exactly the same. When we say that someone "makes the same mistakes over and over again" this may be largely so, but those mistakes are never *exactly* the same ones. As another great Greek thinker said, time is like a river (and we may say, life is a pilgrimage) in which no one can ever put his foot in the same place.

* Throughout his life, Harry S. Truman remembered having read him

(That word did not exist in his time; it is only relatively recently that we have come to consider biography as history.) His portraits of famous and infamous Greeks and Romans are most readable and inspiring even now. But there is one great difference that separates Plutarch from every modern biographer. When Plutarch describes, for example, the Emperor Tiberius, he describes him in the way he was, including certain acts during his reign; but he writes nothing about how Tiberius had come to be that way; he writes almost nothing about his childhood and his adolescence— in sum, about his *becoming*. In this sense it is not psychoanalysis but our *historical consciousness* that has taken another step forward—in the sense of being profoundly aware of *becoming* and not only of *being*.

This kind of historical consciousness was only dormant during the Middle Ages. There *were* important historians then, too, but many of them were *chroniclers* rather than historians. They and their masters found it important to record what happened and when*—but were seldom in-

---

in high school—our last president with such a classical education or, rather, with a *memory* of a classical education.

* *When!* That is something that you must *always* keep in mind. Yes, history is more than a list of dates; but *when* something happened (or

spired by a finely developed critical sense. And then came the Renaissance, with a suddenly flourishing of interest in history, inspired by an admiration of all that was grand and fine in Greece and Rome. (Consider that more people in Europe spoke and read Latin in 1500 than in 1000 A.D.—a fact unknown to those who think that Latin has been a "dead" language for ages).* But, in an important way, the Renaissance respect and admiration for men and things past were still inadequate. They *idealized* the Greeks and the Romans, with a kind of idealization that was often insufficiently historical—though not without grand results of their own.**

Here are a few examples of the difference between our

----

someone lived) may be the most important component of their reality. As a matter of fact, it is indispensable. Julian Marías (a Spanish philosopher) wrote: "We cannot understand the meaning of what a man says unless we know *when* he said it and *when* he lived. Until quite recently, one could read a book or contemplate a painting without knowing the exact period during which it was brought into being…. Today…all undated reality seems vague and invalid, having the insubstantial form of a ghost."

* So it is conceivable that after a long disappearance of book printing and book reading, hundreds of years from now more people may actually print and buy and read books—Shakespeare's sonnets or Balzac's novels, for example—than do now.

** This is worth keeping in mind, especially nowadays. The Renaissance began, in many ways, with an emulation of Greek and Roman forms of consciousness and that of the greatest thinkers, writers, and masters of art four hundred years ago. Shakespeare's attraction to and interest in history was already amazing. Consider his many plays about kings of England. Yet in his famous Globe Theater the most ancient of kings or Romans were dressed in his contemporary, that is Elizabethan, robes and costumes. Or: when Titian or Raphael painted Biblical scenes, their immortal paintings show figures dressed in sixteenth-century Italian clothes, and in the background there are villas and carriages typical of sixteenth-century Italy. But then, less than two hundred years later, even the most amateurish theatricals would drape Caesar or Marc Antony in some kind of a toga; and the classical landscapes of a Rembrandt or a Poussin will represent Joseph or Mary or Herod in biblical costumes.*

That is a mark of our then-developing *historical con-*

---

art, especially painting, sculpture, and architecture; then the Renaissance craftsmen went on, far beyond emulation, achieving masterpieces of their own. For all art, indeed, all human creation (including the writing of history) must *begin* with emulation, with a wish to imitate the finished achievements of great masters.

* Surely we do not expect to see George Washington represented as riding in an automobile. That is an *anachronism*—according to the dictionary, "anything existing or represented out of date"—a word that first appeared in English only about three centuries ago.

sciousness, which is a sudden evolution of the Western mind as important (and as profound) as the evolution of the scientific method in the sixteenth and seventeenth centuries. The latter resulted in an entirely new view of the Earth's (and of man's) place in the universe. The former resulted in recognizing a new dimension of human consciousness. One example (or, rather, symptom) of this new kind of consciousness was the appearance of the word "primitive" in English, French, and other Western European languages about four hundred years ago. It marked a new concept of evolution (or even of education)—indeed, of "progress." To the Greeks, for example, "barbarian" meant people who lived outside Greece, beyond Greek civilization. It was a designation of certain people in a certain place, rather than at a certain time. But the word "primitive" obviously designates people who are *behind* us in time, rather than beyond us in space. And then, in the seventeenth century, especially in France, England, and Holland, this new sense of progress and of historical evolution multiplies. It is there in the appearance of a spate of new words, for example "century," "age," "modern"—words that either did not exist before or that had then acquired an entirely new meaning. ("Century," for example, before about 1650 had meant only a military unit of one hundred men.) And it was only toward the end of the seventeenth century that some people began to look back and call the Middle Ages the Middle Ages.

There are two matters to consider about this. First, in the Middle Ages people did *not* know that they lived during, or even near the end of, the Middle Ages—whereas we know that we are living at the end of the Modern Age.* Second, the notion of the "Modern" (meaning: today's) Age reflected a certain kind of enlightened optimism, meaning that this "Modern" Age would last and progress forever; that, even through many difficulties, things (and probably human nature, too) were bound to get better and better all the time. We have (or ought to have) a more chastened view about that; but it is more and more obvious that the so-called Modern Age itself is a recognizable historical pe-

---

* A definite symptom of our present consciousness of history is our knowledge that we live near the end, or even at the end, of an age. (A phrase such as "It's like the end of the Roman Empire" may be understood or even spoken by many an unschooled man or woman today, when confronted with a particularly ugly example of moral decay.) The Romans of the fourth or fifth centuries A.D. knew that many things had gone wrong and that matters were so much better in the time of their grandparents, but none of them thought that what was happening to them was something like what had happened to the Assyrians or Egyptians or Greeks.

riod, one approximately from 1500 to 2000 A.D. (hence, its very designation, "Modern," may eventually change in the language of our descendants).

This growing consciousness of history went apace with a growing interest in history. That, in the eighteenth century, led to more and more fine books about history, to the extent that we may generalize about history having become in that century a branch of literature. Probably the greatest example of this development was Edward Gibbon who, suddenly inspired in Rome by his view of the sunken monuments of the Roman Forum, decided to re-search and write a monumental book. The result, *The Decline and Fall of the Roman Empire*, remains to this day not only one of the greatest histories ever written but, even more, an enduring monument of English prose literature. Besides that tremendous achievement it must be noted that while Gibbon was not a professional historian (he lived just before the beginning of professional historianship), he was historian enough to rely on original Latin sources, which he would amply cite in his footnotes. There are many things in the Gibbonian interpretations that we have come to see differently; but there can be no question that two hundred or more years ago he exemplified a new sense of history, when a wide spreading of historical interest and of historical consciousness was in the air. Symptoms and examples of this were so numerous that there is no space here to detail them or even to sum them up.*

One (but only one) example of this burgeoning interest in history was the birth of professional historianship in Germany, which resulted in the first academic degree in history established by the University of Göttingen around 1777: the first Ph.D. in history, a university doctorate. One hundred years later this concept and practice of professional historianship had spread around the world. By 1900 there were very few nations where universities did not grant a Ph.D. in history. In sum, whereas in the eighteenth century history was regarded as literature, in the nineteenth century it had become a Science. This was mostly (though not exclusively) the achievement of German historians. The results were enormous. The position—and the recognition—of the professional historian was born. The methods of professional historianship became established: the insistence on "primary" sources, the requirements of seminars and of doc-

---

* Consider the estimable knowledge of ancient history by our Founders, who used much of that knowledge in mulling over the drafting of the new Constitution of the United States.

toral dissertations, monographs, bibliographies, footnotes, professional journals. Great historians, in every country, produced astonishingly learned and detailed works, shedding light into some of the remotest recesses of history. All of this went together with the general interest in history in a century when, among other things, the historical novel was born, and when architecture tended to emulate many historic styles. By the end of the century there was hardly anyone who would question the famous phrase of the German historian Leopold von Ranke, that the historian's task was to reconstruct a past event "wie es eigentlich gewesen," "as it really was." Indeed, most people accepted the professional historians' claim to Objective History; as the great English historian Lord Acton said, civilization was now able to produce, say, a history of the Battle of Waterloo that would not only be acceptable to present and future English and French and Prussian historians but that would be complete and definite and perfect—because of its objectivity, and because of the rigor of the scientific method of its research.

One hundred years later thinking historians do not share such an optimistic belief. We must recognize that history, by its very nature, is "revisionist." To put it in other terms, history, unlike law, tries its subjects through multiple jeopardy. History is the frequent, and constant, rethinking of the past. There may be 1,000 biographies of Abraham Lincoln, but there is no reason to doubt (indeed, it is almost certain) that sooner or later there will be a 1,001st one, with something new in its contents, and not necessarily because of new materials that its author had found, but because of his new viewpoint.* In any case, the general cultural and civilizational crisis of the twentieth century has also reached the historical profession. While in the eighteenth century history was seen as a branch of literature, and in the nineteenth as a branch of science, for the twentieth century we cannot make such a summary statement. One general tendency, which most historians accept or at least share, is the view of history as a form of social science. This does not merely mean the application of such "disciplines" as sociology, economics, geography, and psychology to history, but the recognition that history cannot be exclusively, or per-

---

* The view that the great cathedral of history is being built brick by brick by historians, some of them filling gaps and forming pillars, while the majority of them add their small bricks in the form of monographs (a monograph is a work dealing with a single subject) or even monographic doctoral dissertations, is not entirely a wrong one—but we must recognize that the greatest of cathedrals are never finished; they are in constant need of cleaning and of refurbishing, indeed, of all kinds of repairs—and also that every generation may see them differently.

haps not even primarily, the history of politics and of wars and of rulers (as the English historian Sir John Seeley said around 1880, "History is past politics, and politics is present history"); it must deal with the lives and records of large masses of people. Another tendency is to recognize history as a predominant form of thought—as, for example, the American philosopher William James put it: "You can give humanistic value to almost anything by teaching it histori-cally. Geology, economics, mechanics, are humanities when taught with reference to the successive achievements of the geniuses to which these sciences owe their being. Not taught thus, literature remains grammar, art a catalogue, history a list of dates, and natural science a sheet of formulas and weights and measures." In other words, "Science" did not and does not exist without scientists; and the history of science is the history of scientists and of their achievements. Thus Science is a part of history, rather than the reverse: for in the history of the world, Nature came first, and then came Man, and only then the Science of Nature.*

---

* One of the significant developments of the twentieth century has been the appearance of historians and of the Western methods of historical research among peoples who had been previously unacquainted them. For, until very recently, history has been a particularly Western form of inquiry and of exposition. The richest chronicles of Indian or

PROFESSIONAL HISTORY

❧

WE HAVE NOW SEEN that the appearance and the recognition of the professional historian—of a man or a woman with a Ph.D. in history—is a relatively recent phenomenon. Among the great nations of the world, England was the only one whose universities in 1900 did not grant such degrees (because of the then uniquely British high degree of the M.A.), but soon after 1900 they adopted this practice too. This qualifying of professionals has had of course many positive results. Since this essay is written not for graduate but undergraduate students, I must sum them up briefly.

In our American system the vast majority of students who, either by obligation or by choice, take a history course in college do not go on to study history further in graduate schools. This is also true of students who major in history. The training of professional historians begins in various

---

Chinese or Japanese culture are legends and chronicles, not histories: they are devoid of the critical sense of a Thucydides. (One exception is the Arab Ibn Khaldoon.) As late as a century ago, a Japanese or Chinese or Indian wishing to read something fairly accurate and particular of the recent history of his country had to rely on histories of his country written by European or English or American historians. This is no longer so.

graduate schools. There, at most after a year or so, they must decide in what "fields" or "periods" they wish to specialize: American? European? Ancient? Renaissance? Modern? etc. They must take certain methodological courses and seminars. In the latter, they work under the guidance of one of their professors, a specialist in his "field." This kind of apprenticeship must, in the end, lead to their selection (with their professor's approval) of a limited topic that has not been researched or treated before in detail. They must research and write a monographic dissertation of it. This must be accepted by their professor and later "defended" before a faculty committee (defending a thesis is at times not more than a formality), after which they will be granted their Ph.D. This kind of graduate period may last as few as three and as many as ten years, depending on many circumstances. After obtaining this degree, our new professional historians are qualified to apply for college or university teaching positions, or for other occupations that nowadays require an advanced professional historian's degree (government, museums, publishing, public or private archives, etc.).

The origin of all of these procedures was German, including that of the apprenticeship. Like all university institutions, including apprenticeships, they are of course all too liable to vagaries, fashions, academic politics, ideologies, and personal intrigues among the faculty. The historical profession, no more and no less than other professions, is not immune to the intrusion of ideological fads such as Psychohistory or Feminist History or Multiculturalism. There are many sorry examples of these, especially in our times. Yet, by and large, this originally nineteenth-century and German-designed training cannot be abandoned—that is, not until a radically new system of education and of higher learning, involving a new need for new kinds of certified teachers comes about, something that is not likely in the immediate future.

There is, however, one overwhelming argument against a thoughtless acceptance of the professionalization (and of the consequent bureaucratization) of history. It is that there is *no essential difference* between the "professional" and the "amateur" historian (just as there is no difference between a person and a historical person, or between a source and a historical source). No one would prefer to undergo brain surgery at the hands of someone who is not qualified as a professional brain surgeon. But many of the greatest historians, not only before but also since the nineteenth century, were men and women who did not possess the Ph.D. To say that you cannot be a historian unless you have a Ph.D. in history is not quite as absurd as to say that you cannot be a poet unless you have a Ph.D. in poetry—but there is at least a touch of absurdity in it. We are, all, historians by nature while we are scientists only by choice; and history is not A Science. (Or, as the English historian Veronica Wedgwood said in her aphorism: "History is an art—like all the other sciences.") The writing of a first-class history (or biography) is open to anyone who has thoroughly read everything he could find about his topic; who has an ability to express himself clearly; and who is mature enough to understand some things about human nature itself—three general requirements that, then, depend on the very authenticity and quality of his interest. His main interest must be history, rather than the positioning of his historianship.

THE METHODS OF HISTORY

ONE OF THE GREATEST of professional historians, the German Theodor Mommsen, wrote more than one hundred years ago: "The elements of the historical discipline cannot be learned, for every man is endowed with them." The (probably even greater) Swiss Jakob Burckhardt said to his students that there is no such thing as a historical method. *Bisogna saper leggere*, he said (in Italian): "You must know how to read." And by this of course he did not mean speed-reading or other devices, but that you must acquire the practice and particular quality of your reading.

Yes, strictly speaking history has no method. (Some academic historians will not like to hear that, since that may seem to reduce their achievement of their degree and of their expertise. Ignore them.) A main reason for this is that history has no technical jargon, it has no language of its own: history is written, spoken, and taught in our everyday languages. (It is also thus that you cannot be a good historian if you are not a capable writer.) You must know how to read; but also how to express what you know. That expression is not merely the packaging of your knowledge; it is the content itself. (Every human expression is not just the packaging of a thought, but its completion.)

There are, however, some limitations. History is the knowledge that human beings have of other human beings; and every human life is unique. Theodore Roosevelt was not merely the twenty-sixth president of the United States, or a President Type A. He was Theodore Roosevelt, born in 1858, died in 1919. As unique as your great-grandmother, the jolly and rotund Mrs. Myrtle Brown, 1902-1987.

There are a few small methods, or "tricks," to historical study and writing, as there are of any human endeavor, such as cleaning or cooking. They can hardly be avoided. As with cooking, you must know where to begin: you must know what you want—indeed, what you'd like—to cook. After that, go to a cookbook. You must know what subject or theme or period or person interests you. After that, there are bibliographies (general and specific ones, and others at the ends of books already written about your topic), guides, encyclopedias, etc., leading you to more reading material. Nowadays this is made easier through various programs on the Internet; but none of that will spare you from the—we hope, interesting—task of reading which is, really, what most of "re-search" may mean. There are also historical journals, (often quarterlies), with articles and book reviews and bibliographies in every "field."*

---

* No matter how detailed and assiduous, your research will never be complete. The nineteenth-century monographic ideal was that certifiable historian who, having read every document and every writing relating to his topic, is able to produce a *complete* and *definitive* history of it. This is no longer possible—because of the possibility that new documents, new treatments, and more publications about his topic, many in different places and languages of the world, may yet appear. (Of course some histories are more "definitive" than others. But never absolutely so.)

After a while you will have gathered an amount of material. That will usually fall into three categories. Some of this you will not use (it is a great mistake to use *everything*). Some of this you will use. Some of the latter will be extraneous to your text, belonging in a footnote. Roughly speaking there are only two kinds of footnotes: one that *must* give the *exact* reference of where your quotation or material comes from; the other, an illustration or explanation of something that may be interesting or significant as an "aside," worth mentioning, though not within the particular paragraph of your main text.

About these methods—including much more than a description of "methods"—see the superb book entitled *The Modern Researcher*, by Jacques Barzun and Henry A. Graff, now in its umpteenth edition. (Better: buy it. You will be able to use it for the rest of your life, whether you become a historian or not.) Now note that the title of this superb handbook is not *The Modern History-Writer* but *The Modern Researcher.* The reason is that this book is a guide not only for history students but for *anyone* writing a paper in *any* discipline. Yes, you will find footnotes and bibliographies not only in history books and articles, but in such various places as *The Journal of Ophthalmology* or *Musical*

Instruments of Turkey or *The Physiology of the African Gnu*—
because this practice of footnotes and bibliography (which
some people call "a scientific apparatus") was adopted by *all*
other disciplines in the nineteenth century, emulating the
then-developed methods of professional historiography.* In
this respect—at least in the method of authentication—all
scientific literature follows the historical method now.

There is, finally, one important rule that the nineteenth-
century German historians established: their distinction between "primary" and "secondary" sources, the first being
"original," the second not. Example: a personal letter by
Theodore Roosevelt telling Mrs. Roosevelt that she ought
to hire a new maid is a primary source; a relation of this
event in a book or article entitled *The Roosevelts' Household*

---

* Note this word: historiography. Its literal meaning: the writing of
history. Thus, strictly speaking, a Ph.D. in history should really be
named a Ph.D. in historiography. But no: because in our minds and
languages, *historiography* and *history* and *story* overlap. (In the Latin
languages, for example, *story* and *history* are the same words.) Yes,
because history essentially means telling a story, being (as we saw on the
first page of this essay) descriptive, rather than definitive, while historiography is the study of what others have written about this or that
historical topic.

Allow me to give a personal example. My recent (1997) book *The
Hitler of History* is a critical study of the historians and biographers who

in the White House is a secondary one. This distinction is important and ought to be observed (for example, almost all Ph.D. dissertations in history require research in at least some "primary" sources).* Yet it is no longer as ironbound as it once seemed—because communications in the twentieth century (letters signed but not written by important people; telephonic and other communications) tend to wash away the once rigid line between "primary" and "secondary" sources.

What matters, first and foremost, is the genuineness of your interest in history—almost no matter what history. And this is as true of undergraduates as it is of graduate students. This leads to the relatively new advantages of history majors. A history major who does not go on to graduate school has lately become prized by intelligent employers, since they know that a history major is not some kind

----

have written about Hitler. But it is, inevitably, a study of Hitler himself, too. Thus (a) it is both a historiographical and historical work; and (b) its main subject is that of problems, rather than that of periods—but the latter is true of much of history, always.

* Keep in mind that just as a small book or painting or sculpture or building is not necessarily inferior to large ones, a research paper with an impressive number of footnotes is not necessarily better than one with few footnotes (or even one with none).

of apprentice archivist, but someone who knows how to read and write relatively well—and whose knowledge of some history gives him at least a modicum of understanding of the variety of human beings. History is, as I wrote earlier, the knowledge that human beings have of other human beings, a kind of knowledge more valuable and, yes, even more practical, than the knowledge human beings have of more primitive organisms and of things.

THE INTEREST IN HISTORY

AT THE END of this century—indeed, for some decades now—we are witnessing a dual development. Many people know *less* history than their parents or grandparents had known; but *more* people are interested in history than probably ever before. On the one hand, less history is being required and taught in our schools than earlier in this century.* At the same time there exists an appetite for history

---

* In our colleges and universities, too, the requirements and sometimes the very content of historical study have declined. This includes the tendency to emphasize what is sometimes inadequately called "social history," at times amounting to hardly more than a retrospective and shortsighted sociologizing, something that inspires little interest in students.

throughout the world—particularly in the United States—
that has no precedents.* There are so many evidences of this
that I can list only a few. For example, while few history
courses are required in high schools and colleges, in *all*
colleges history courses are among the first of elective—that
is non-required—courses chosen by students. There are
history programs and the History Channel on television,
historical films, historical "documentaries" and "docudramas,"
obviously responding to the interests of millions, dealing
with topics that were hardly featured as late as two genera-
tions ago. Within commercial publishing, popular histories
are outselling novels for the first time in 200 years. It is now
accepted that serious biographies belong to history; biographies sell very well, while the very methods of serious
biographers have become entirely historical. There exist
popular historical magazines, even about specialized periods,
that have a readership more solid and widespread than that
of most other magazines. There are three times as many local
historical societies as there were sixty years ago; their membership includes many young people, not predominantly

---

* In the 1920s, Henry Ford proclaimed, "History is bunk," and Herbert
Hoover's Secretary of Commerce said, "Tradition is the enemy of
Progress." No "conservatives" (or even "liberals") think that way now.

old ladies in tennis shoes whose interest is primarily genea-logical. The historical appetite of Americans has become unprecedented and large. Of course it is served, and will continue to be served, with plenty of junk food. Of that professional historians may be aware. (Yet the existence of this appetite for history is unknown to many of them.) Around 1980 the extraordinary English thinker Owen Barfield wrote: "The Western outlook emphasizes the importance of *history* and pays an ever increasing attention to it...there is a new concept of *history* in the air, a new feeling for its true significance. We have witnessed the dim dawning of a sense that history is to be grasped as something substantial to the being of man, as an 'existential encounter.'"

And now, moving from the recognition of this univer-sal and national growth of interest in history, I must say something about *your* interest. Someone who does not know how to cook must depend on a cookbook; but be-fore opening the cookbook he must have an appetite. That interest—that appetite—must be recognized, nurtured, and cultivated. It comes not from the outside, but from the inside—as all human appetites and interests do. When you are interested in something—whether it is the taste of a good glass of wine, the sound of a certain kind of music, or

a certain book—you must not only recognize it but liter-
ally *keep it in your mind* and follow it up, making the effort
to find another kind of that particular wine, or another record
of that particular composer, or another book by the same
author, or yet another dealing with the same topic or a similar one. That effort will be worth all the trouble (if trouble
it is), because that is how the human mind works—different from the laws of natural science. The more you know
about something (and about something that really interests
you), the easier it will be for you to absorb more knowledge about it. When a sack or a box is full, it becomes more
and more difficult to force more stuff into it. But when we
really know something (and especially when we are interested in something), it is easier not only to absorb but to
know and understand and remember more and more things
about it. In sum, the *quality* of your interest will not only
enrich your mind; it will govern the very *quantity* of your
knowledge. And that is true of historical knowledge, the
knowledge of the past—which, in a way, is the fundament
of just about all of the human knowledge we have.*

---

* Perhaps the Greeks sensed that, too: for them, Memory was the mother
of all the Muses.

John Lukacs

THE GREATNESS OF
HISTORICAL LITERATURE
 ❧

TO DIRECT YOU NOW TO, or even to list, the greatest of
histories is almost impossible, for one simple reason: in one
way or another *all* literature is, to a great extent, historical.
It is quite possible—and there is nothing wrong with this—
that your interest in history may have been stimulated by a
movie or by a television play or by a novel. The varieties of
historical literature are enormous.* One word about the
novel may be in order here. The novel is a relatively new
form of literature. It appeared in the eighteenth century,
together with the evolution of our historical consciousness,
and around the same time that professional history was
born. (I am not referring to "historical novels"—a later
phenomenon and one now rather past.) Novels such as Jane
Austen's *Pride and Prejudice,* or William Makepeace
Thackeray's *Vanity Fair,* or Arnold Bennett's *The Old*

---

* *The Varieties of History* (New York, 1956; revised 1973), edited by Fritz
Stern, is another excellent book to have. It deals with the various
writings of historians about history itself. Strictly speaking, its contents
deal with the varieties of historiography.

Wives' Tale, or Honoré de Balzac's *Old Goriot,* or Thomas Mann's *Buddenbrooks,* or F. Scott Fitzgerald's *The Great Gatsby* do not tell us only a story; they do not only remind us of many everlasting truths about human beings and about their inclinations;* they tell us, plausibly, how *certain* men and women, in a *certain* place, and *at a certain time* (!) lived and talked and thought and desired and believed. So does a good biography, of course.

But this booklet is *A Student's Guide to the Study of History.* So here is a very incomplete and random list of some of the greatest historians whose writings you may find and should eventually read. Many of them should be available in paperbound editions; all of them are available in any decent library. But from time to time you should buy some of them for yourself, and not only for purposes of a history course or a research paper or essay. You must begin to enrich your own library, a personal library that is not merely a collection of once acquired books—that is, remnants—but of books that you will read—and perhaps reread again.

---

* The French writer Guy de Maupassant (1850-1893) said: The aim of the realistic novel "is not to tell a story, to amuse us or to appeal to our feelings, but to compel us to reflect, and to understand the darker and deeper meaning of events."

SOME OF THE GREATEST HISTORIANS

This is *not* a bibliography or a bibliographical essay. There are at least three reasons for this. The first is that the mass of writings about history is so enormous that, except for very limited periods or areas or fields of study, not even a selective bibliography will do. The second is that many of the greatest books about a particular people or place or period were not written by historians, and this list contains only the names and main works of historians. The third is that this booklet is a *guide* to the study of history, and not to history *in toto*. (Consider here the difference between a guide to the study of literature—difficult but manageable—and a bibliographical guide to all literature: nonsense—a guide to everything that has ever been written by men and women?)

Ancients

Herodotus (c. 484-425 B.C.) was—somewhat exaggeratedly, but not without substance—sometimes called "the Father of History." He was born under Persian rule, but was thoroughly Greek in every respect; in a sense he was to history (a word that he brought into wide circulation) what Homer had been to the epic. He widely read and traveled; he wrote very well and was perhaps the first writer to demonstrate the critical qualification of a historian. This kind of style and substance is there in his *The Persian Wars*. That critical sense —allied with an impatience for legends and untruths, together with not only great learning but a wise experience of human nature—was next exemplified by **Thucydides** (ca. 471-399 B.C.) in his *History of the Peloponnesian War*, of which he was a contemporary and participant (for a short time he served as a general). His style and his analysis of human nature are exceptional and at the time very new. A generation later, the great speaker Demosthenes was supposed to have said that he learned everything from Thucydides. **Xenophon** (c. 430-355 B.C.) was a conservative Athenian, a participant in a great military campaign across Asia Minor, whence his nearly immortal *Anabasis* (and the rarely known but also splendid *The Hellenica*), a thrilling history of his times. His style was plain and direct, like that of Julius Caesar (see below), whom he influenced.

The "bridge" between the Greek and Roman historians is **Polybius** (c. 204-122 B.C.),* a Greek who lived under Ro-

---

*A frivolous remark. Look at the dates of these ancient historians, at a time when the human life span was about forty years long. There is this tendency for historians to live for a remarkably long time! Of course there are exceptions. But there is no exception to the rule that no good history was ever written by an immature person!

man rule and who wrote and traveled much (as a matter of fact he accompanied Scipio to the siege of Carthage). He wrote thirty-nine books, of which five survive. They deal with Roman history, including the Romans' conquest of Greece and then of Carthage. He was a tireless researcher and somewhat verbose; but he influenced the Roman historians directly, even though all of the latter were but individual successors to the Greek "founders of history."

These great Roman historians lived and wrote mostly during the dramatic age when Rome changed from republic to empire. **Livy** (Titus Livius, 59 B.C.-17 A.D.) wrote his long—but very readable—*History of Rome* from the very beginnings of the city to the then present. He was a Roman aristocrat who often insisted that the purpose of history is to teach us something by contemplating examples of morality.* Only about one-third of his writings survive, but he had written very much and continues to be an invaluable source for the early history of Rome. **Julius Caesar's** (100-

---

* Livy was not alone in this. All great historians incline to such a recognition, through all ages. His forerunner Dionysius Halicarnassus (first century B.C.), a Greek philosopher, said: "History is philosophy, teaching by example." This was repeated by Lord Bolingbroke, the English statesman, word for word in the early eighteenth century.

44 B.C.) *Commentaries*, including *The Gallic War*, are classics: easily readable accounts by a statesman and general who was also an excellent writer and historian of his own times (two thousand years later his equivalent is Winston Churchill, about whom below). **Pliny the Elder** (c. 23-79 A.D.) wrote many books, but he is not comparable to his nephew **Pliny the Younger** (61-113 A.D.), whose superbly—and easily—readable books include his description of the catastrophic eruption of Vesuvius and the destruction of Pompeii in 79 B.C., during which his uncle perished. By that time we may observe a shift of emphasis of Roman historians toward biography (even though that word did not yet exist), particularly of the lives of successive emperors. This biographical talent is evident in the—again, very readable—*Parallel Lives* of **Plutarch** (46-120 A.D.), another Greek who was a Roman subject, comparing the lives of great Greek and Roman personages and rulers. His contemporary was **Tacitus** (c. 55-117 A.D.), whose *Twelve Annals* deals mostly with imperial Rome during the first century A.D., but who is best known for his *Germania*, an excellent description of the Germanic tribes, their habits and lives, and contemporary histories north of the Alps. The *Twelve Caesars* of **Suetonius** (c. 75-160 A.D.) are often amus-

ing as well as shocking, containing scandalous and racy stories about the lives of successive, and sometimes very different, emperors of Rome.

These excellent men were followed by hundreds of Roman historians during the last four centuries of the Roman empire and by many thousands of others who have written about Greece and Rome during the last two thousand years. But now comes a change: we must, by necessity, limit this short essay to the names of those who were no longer contemporaries of the times of which they wrote, but whose books illuminate the past in incomparable and novel ways. Their works are the results of the new phase of *historical consciousness*—a step beyond historical thinking, about which evolution I wrote earlier. A classic example is **Edward Gibbon** (1737-1794), whose *Decline and Fall of the Roman Empire* is unique because of its imaginative qualities, the splendor of its English style, and Gibbon's thorough reliance on the ancient writers and sources.

The Middle Ages

When it comes to the Middle Ages, the best introduction to them may be found not in the surviving works of medieval chroniclers, but in the works of twentieth-century historians, such as the Belgian **Henri Pirenne**, a great modern historian of the Dark and Middle Ages, perhaps especially his *Mohammed and Charlemagne* and his short and brilliant *Medieval Cities*. **Eileen Powers** (an English-woman) gave us superb portraits of half a dozen men and women in *Medieval People*, describing their everyday lives. **Johan Huizinga**, a Hollander, perhaps the finest historian who lived in the twentieth century, wrote *The Waning of the Middle Ages*, an extraordinary book encompassing a very new approach of historical description, including his reconstruction of the mental inclinations of people at a certain time.

The Nineteenth Century

We have seen (above, pp. 19-20) that professional history had come into its own in the nineteenth century: its results were protean and wide-ranging. Yet let me mention two men who lived in that century who did *not* wholly share the scientific concept of history but who, in retrospect, emerge as very great writers. One is **Alexis de Tocqueville** (1805-1859), who is mostly known for his classic *Democracy in America* (which is not a history); but his *The Old Regime and the French Revolution* again amounts to a new, and increasingly appreciated, kind of history, penetrating beneath the surface of political events. The Swiss **Jakob Burckhardt** (1818-1897) was perhaps the greatest of historians in the last 200 years, immensely wise and wide-ranging, the founder of modern cultural and art history. His *History of Greek Culture, The Civilization of the Renaissance in Italy, The Age of Constantine the Great*, and his *Judgments on History and Historians* (the latter from recorded notes of his lectures) will still be read centuries from now.

The three classic American historians of the nineteenth century are, first, **Henry Adams** (1838-1918). The last "great" of the Adams family, a direct descendant of two presidents, is mostly known for his *The Education of Henry Adams*, which may remain less enduring than his many brilliant histories, especially *The History of the United States during the Administrations of Jefferson and Madison* (of which abbreviated versions are available). **Francis Parkman** (1823-1893) is the incomparable historian of the French and British empires in North America during the eighteenth century, but also of *The Oregon Trail.* **William H. Prescott** (1796-1859) was the classic historian of the Spanish conquest of the Americas, especially in his *Conquest of Mexico* and *History of the Conquest of Peru*.

The Twentieth Century

When we arrive at histories of the twentieth century written by historians living in the twentieth century, they are innumerable, including the best of them—in many, many languages. But let me single out one great amateur: **Winston Churchill** (1874-1965). All of his books are worth reading, including his six-volume *History of the Second World War*. He loved and revered history. His style is exceptional, and so are his insights. Among other works he wrote a four-volume *History of the English-speaking Peoples*. (And note in this instance the original meaning of the word "amateur," which was not the opposite of a "pro," but someone who loves his subjects and his work.)

One more brief note—about *the philosophy of history*. Many historians (and also other thinkers) have been preoccupied with trying to find a system in history, meaning the coincidence of certain conditions and tendencies recurring at somewhat comparable stages in the histories of different civilizations. The three great twentieth-century names in this regard are the German **Oswald Spengler** (1880-1936), whose *Decline of the West* is a stunning, though erratic, work, reflecting German pessimism about the fate of our civilization after World War I; the Briton **Arnold Toynbee** (1889-

1975), who in his multi-volume *Study of History* attempted to find parallels and similarities in the development of many civilizations; and the English Catholic **Christopher Dawson** (1889-1970), an "amateur" historian of great erudition, who found religion to be the deepest and most enduring element in different civilizations. His assertion of the Christian nature of Europe may be found in many of his scattered volumes, perhaps especially in *The Making of Europe* and *Religion and the Rise of Western Culture*. However, two warnings may be in order here. Reading such philosophies of history may give the reader startling and illuminating generalizations about history in general; but history necessarily consists of particular events, peoples, places, problems, periods. Thus the reading of philosophies of history ought to come *after*, and not *before*, a reader has developed his own interest and preference in reading about particular matters of his own civilization. Also (as Jakob Burckhardt has said), history is not a system, and your own development of a *historical philosophy*—that is, a historical way of looking at and thinking about people, nations, events— ought to precede, and supersede, your interest in *philosophies* of history.

And now a last *however*. There are *no* rules about this,

no rules about reading, *no* rules about what should—or will—interest you. What you must do is follow and feed your own interests—through which practice (and pleasure) you will acquire what Burckhardt named as the *only* historical method: *You must know how to read.*

Let me end with two great statements about what happens if you do *not* have an interest in history. One, ancient, is from Cicero: "To be ignorant of what happened before you were born is to remain a child always." The other, modern, is from the fine American essayist Agnes Repplier: "I used to think that ignorance of history meant only a lack of cultivation and a loss of pleasure. Now I am sure that such ignorance impairs our judgment by impairing our understanding, by depriving us of standards or the power of contrast, and the right to estimate." And, "We can know nothing of any nation unless we know its history."

EMBARKING ON A LIFELONG PURSUIT OF KNOWLEDGE?

*Take Advantage of These New Resources
& a New Website*

⌒〰⌒

The ISI Guides to the Major Disciplines are part of the Intercollegiate Studies Institute's (ISI) **Student Self-Reliance Project**, an integrated, sequential program of educational supplements designed to guide students in making key decisions that will enable them to acquire an appreciation of the accomplishments of Western civilization.

Developed with fifteen months of detailed advice from college professors and students, these resources provide advice in course selection and guidance in actual coursework. The Project elements can be used independently by students to navigate the existing university curriculum in a way that deepens their understanding of our Western intellectual heritage. As indicated below, the Project's integrated components will answer key questions at each stage of a student's education.

What are the strengths and weaknesses of the most selective schools?
Choosing the Right College directs prospective college students to the best and worst that top American colleges have to offer.

What is the essence of a liberal arts education?
A Student's Guide to Liberal Learning will introduce students to the vital connection between liberal education and political liberty.

What core courses should every student take?
A Student's Guide to the Core Curriculum will instruct students how to build their own core curriculum, utilizing electives available at virtually every university, and how to identify and overcome contemporary political biases in those courses.

How can students learn from the best minds in their major field of study?
Study Guides to the Major Disciplines will introduce students to overlooked and misrepresented classics, facilitating work within their majors. Guides currently in production assess the fields of literature, political philosophy, European and American history, and economics.

Which great modern thinkers are neglected?
The Library of Modern Thinkers will introduce students to great minds who have contributed to the literature of the West and who are neglected or denigrated in today's classroom. Figures who make up this series include Robert Nisbet, Eric Voegelin, Wilhelm Roepke, Ludwig von Mises, Will Herberg, and many more.

In order to address the academic problems faced by every student in an ongoing manner, a new website, **www.collegeguide.org**, was recently launched. It offers easy access to unparalleled resources for making the most of one's college experience—and it features an interactive component that will allow students to pose questions about academic life on America's college campuses.

These features make ISI a one-stop organization for serious students of all ages. Visit **www.isi.org** or call **1-800-526-7022** and consider adding your name to the 50,000-plus ISI membership list of teachers, students, and professors.